Messy Moose

By Lois Bick

Illustrated by Ann Iosa

Sadlier-Oxford
A Division of William H. Sadlier, Inc.
New York, NY 10005-1002

Messy Moose tries to be so neat.

But no matter what,
he makes a mess.

He makes a mess with milk.

He makes a mess with mud.

He makes a mess
with markers.

He makes a mess
with meatballs.

But Messy Moose
always cleans up!